PERSIAN
MINIATURES

PERSIAN MINIATURES

From Ancient Manuscripts

INTRODUCTION BY
BASIL GRAY

A MENTOR-UNESCO ART BOOK

PUBLISHED BY
THE NEW AMERICAN LIBRARY OF WORLD LITERATURE, INC.
BY ARRANGEMENT WITH UNESCO

FIRST PRINTING, SEPTEMBER, 1962

MENTOR TRADEMARK REG. U. S. PAT. OFF. AND FOREIGN COUNTRIES
REGISTERED TRADEMARK—MARCA REGISTRADA

MENTOR-UNESCO ART BOOKS ARE PUBLISHED BY
THE NEW AMERICAN LIBRARY OF WORLD LITERATURE, INC.
501 MADISON AVENUE, NEW YORK 22, NEW YORK

PRINTED IN ITALY BY AMILCARE PIZZI S.P.A. MILANO

The miniatures here reproduced belong to two of the greatest periods in the history of the Persian school: the Timurid and the Safavi. The Timurid school of painting was not the creation of Timur himself (d. 1405), one of the greatest conquerors that the world has known, but of his grandsons. Among them the first great patron was Iskandar Sultan, son of Ulugh Beg, who ruled over Fars from the capital, Shiraz, until 1414. He was succeeded by his cousin Ibrahim Sultan, also remembered as a patron, but soon eclipsed by his own younger brother, Baysunghur, who was able to attract all the best artists to his library in Herat until his premature death from dissipation in 1433. Thereafter the Timurid house produced no notable patron of art and letters until the accession at Herat of Sultan Husayn Bayqara (born 1439) in 1468. With his vizier Mir Ali Shir, himself a poet of distinction, he patronized Bihzad, the greatest name in Persian painting, the poet Jami, and the historian Khwandamir. It is doubtful whether his artistic patronage was exercised effectively before about 1485.

In this volume are reproduced miniatures from two of the most famous Timurid manuscripts and a double-page composition which has long been associated with the name of Bihzad.

The Imperial Library. Gulistan, Teheran.

Kalila and Dimna (1420-1425). The two doves (detail).

1. The Shah-Nama of Baysunghur

One of these manuscripts was without question produced in Baysunghur's royal scriptorium, and copied by his master calligrapher, Ja'far; it was finished in January 1430, less than two years after the new text of the great Persian epic *Shah-nama*, or Book of King, was established under Baysunghur's personal supervision. It contains the prince's preface, thereafter prefixed to many copies. In his long poem, Firdawsi crystallized the traditions of the Persians about their own past, from mythological beginnings to the end of the historic Sassanian dynasty. A splendid ornamental rosette on the opening page carries the ex-libris of the prince. Mainly executed in blue and gold but with touches of red and green, the title pages shown the genius of the Persians for abstract design, which was also displayed in stucco, wall tiles and textiles, but nowhere so richly as in manuscript illumination. A double-page pictorial frontispiece follows (here reproduced), then twenty miniatures, which occupy the greater part of the full page.

The frontispiece (Plates 1 and 2) does not illustrate the poem, but instead depicts the patron Baysunghur in the hunting field watching the conclusion of a battue in which his courtiers are slaughtering deer, wolves, a bear, and a lioness, while he is being refreshed by a cup of the wine of which he was so fond. It had become the custom to prefix to books prepared for royal patrons such pictures of royal occupations as a variant on the earlier tradition of the hieratic portrait of the sovereign on his throne, surrounded by his court; or being offered by the author or copyist the manuscript itself. The patron was now depicted in a lively and personal way, so that this may be accepted as a true portrait of Baysunghur, the aesthete and dilettante.

The fourth miniature depicts the foolish king, Kay Ka'us, of the legendary Kayanian line, soon after his accession, listening to the praises of the country of Mazandaran, by a wandering minstrel who is really a Div (devil) in disguise, sent to lure the king to make an attack on the stronghold of the Divs in that country (Plate 3). All the costumes and accessories are contemporary with the manuscript, and the blue and white flasks on the table witness to the fashion in fifteenth century Persia for Chinese porcelain decorated in blue on a white slip ground under a colorless glaze. Gold is freely used as an alternative to blue in the skies of Timurid miniatures. It testifies to the power of the burning sun in that largely desert land. (See the French translation of the *Shah-nama* by Jules Mohl, I, p. 385).

The next illustration shows the great Persian hero, Rustam, fighting, against his own grandson Barzu without recognizing him (Plate 4). This incident, obviously modelled on the better-known story of Rustam's fight with his son Suhrab, is an interpolation into the *Shah-nama* from a long poem, the *Barzu-nama*, composed by an unknown author about A.D. 1100. The incident, which ended tragically in the slaying of Barzu, was contrived by the great enemy of Persia, the Turanian king Afrasiab. Rustam is always recognizable by the tiger-skin coat he wears over his plate armor.

The sixth miniature illustrates the tragic end of Siyavush, son of Kay Ka'us, king of Iran, who had become estranged from his father and taken refuge with King Afrasiab, whose daughter he married (Plate 5). After being promoted to great honor he excited the jealousy of the king's brother, Garsivaz, by his strength and skill in the arts of war, and especially with the bow; he is denounced to the king and finally murdered in the most humiliating and brutal way, thus provoking the long war between the Iranians and Turanians (see Mohl, II, p. 326).

One of the episodes of this war is the series of battles of the Twelve Rukhs or champions of Iran and Turan, of which the last is depicted in the ninth miniature (Plate 6). It shows the end of the Turanian chief, Piran, who is slain by Gudarz. The Turanians wear surcoats of purple over their armor and the artist has shown great skill in massing

*Khamseh of Jami. Sultan Sanjar and the old woman.
End of fifteenth century.*

Muraqqa Gulshan. Miniature from the period of Shah Abbas I (uncertain subject).

so many figures in the small area available to him, the circular shape on the right being especially typical of the compositions in this manuscript. The banners seen against the sky are embroidered with the Chinese motifs of a dragon and lions playing with a ball, as is typical of the applied arts of this period, when intercourse with the Ming court was maintained by embassies from the Timurid princes (see Mohl, III, p. 464).

The eleventh miniature illustrates the first station of the seven to be accomplished by Isfandiyar on the route to reach Arjasp, the tyrant, in his brazen stronghold. He slays two monstrous wolves with horns like stags and tusks like an elephant, which bar his way (Plate 7). The rock-edged desert here is typical of the landscape in this manuscript and far closer to the natural landscape in Iran than could be expected by those who have not seen it. (See Mohl, IV, p. 394).

We next see depicted one of the great romantic moments of the Firdawsi poem (Plate 8), where, in the fifteenth miniature, the artist has shown the slave girl Gulnar looking out of a window of the palace of King Ardawan, whose confidential secretary she was, and seeing and falling in love with Ardashir, at that time in charge of the royal stables. Nonetheless the artist has depicted Ardashir in the costume fitting to a prince, mindful of the fact that the couple were to elope together and establish the great national dynasty of the Sassanians, called after their son Sassan (see Mohl, v, p. 226). The inscription on the tower of the palace reads, "This building was erected by order of the great Sultan Baysunghur," a reminder that this prince was a highly skilled calligrapher and designed the inscriptions on the public buildings which he endowed in Herat.

The last illustration (Plate 9) is taken from the sixteenth miniature and shows King Yazdagird entertaining the Arab King Mundhir of Hira, to whom he is about to entrust the education of his infant son, Bahram Gur, who was thus brought up in manly sports, especially hunting, in which he was to gain such fame. But he was also enabled

12

to learn Arabic and perhaps Greek. In the picture Mundhir, who wears the Arab type of turban and is seated on the left, is being offered a robe of honor held by two girls in the foreground. Many of the miniatures in this book extend into the margins, thus gaining greater spaciousness. (See Mohl, v, p. 369).

2. The Book of Kalila and Dimna

The second early Timurid manuscript from which miniatures have been chosen must also, from its quality and richness, have been produced for a royal patron; but it now lacks both dedication and colophon. Consequently, the date of this copy of the fable book entitled *Kalila and Dimna*, the names of the two jackals who are its heroes, can only be deduced from stylistic criteria. The matter is complicated by the existence, in the Sarayi Library in Istanbul, of Baysunghur's own copy of this book. It was copied for him by Muhammad ibn Hussam, who enjoyed the title of Shams-al-Din, in the same year (A.D. 1430) as the *Shah-nama*, and contains twenty-two miniatures as well as a double-page frontispiece of the finest quality. The miniatures in the Istanbul copy differ from those in the Teheran manuscript by their greater brilliance of coloring and stiffness of drawing, in both respects repeating the stylistic features of the Teheran *Shah-nama* of the same year. There is no doubt that they were produced in the same atelier. The Teheran *Kalila and Dimna* on the other hand excels by its liveliness and delicacy of drawing, and its sensitive use of color.

An anthology produced for Iskandar Sultan in 1410-1411, and now in the Gulbenkian Foundation in Lisbon, contains an illustration of Majnun living in the desert with the wild beasts, in which there are delightfully natural deer comparable with those in the Teheran *Kalila* manuscript. The pleasure shown in depicting flowering trees against a gold sky is evidenced in both volumes. But the *Kalila* is more advanced in variety of composition and above all in psycho-

Jami al-Tavarikh (1596). Oelun, mother of the future Genghis Khan pursues tribes who refuse to obey her (detail).

Jami al-Tavarikh (1596). In flight after a series of defeats. Genghis drinks water squeezed from the mud of a pond (detail).

logical insight into animal life. In sophistication it approaches the work of the school of Baysunghur in Herat, and shares with two manuscripts illustrated there in 1426-1427 both carpet design and the articulation of architectural form as a flat screen across the picture surface, often relieved by half-open doors through which a figure is passing. We may thus ascribe it as a Timurid work of about 1420-1425, produced for a royal patron who, at that date, cannot have been Iskandar or his brother Beyqara, but might be either of their cousins Ibrahim or Baysughur.

The frontispiece (Plates 10 and 11), now damaged and in part repainted, shows the presentation of the completed book to the patron, seated on his throne in a garden court, a favorite setting at all times in Persian art. The prince is still young and the birds in flight on the left page are naturalistically drawn. Below them a servant is pouring wine into a jar through an ingenious type of long-spouted cup. As is often the case, the frontispiece stands rather apart from the rest of the miniatures, partly because it covers two whole pages while the rest of the miniatures are oblong, the height being much less than the width. This gives a different character to the illustration of the presentation of the Sanskrit Fables by their translator, the physician Barzu, to King Anushirwan, in spite of the similarity of the subject depicted (Plate 12). The grouping of the figures is free and asymmetric and we enter at once into the imagined world in which the action of the stories takes place.

The artist of the next two miniatures from this manuscript has the power to open the door on to an imaginary world, with the heightened intensity of poetic insight. They are surely by the same hand. In the first (Plate 13) the four friends, the deer, the crow, the tortoise, and the mouse, are grouped around a pool shaded by lemon and orange trees and bordered by flowering plants, so greatly valued against the background of the nearly bare hillside. In the second (Plate 14) there is indeed violent action, as the old lion springs on the ass, which has been lured there by the

16

jackal, but it is once more the natural setting which is the most vivid part of the picture, here enlivened by the jade-green of the bamboo shoots on the right. This naturalism owes much to the old tradition of flower painting in China, wich had been introduced to Persia by the Mongols in the fourteenth century, and was now fully absorbed into the native Persian romantic world of poetic feeling. With these new means the miniaturists were able to express a childlike vision of the natural world.

The last example from this manuscript (Plate 15) shows the wonderful bird which was the king's favorite, in the form of the old Persian Simurgh, which had figured prominently in the *Shah-nama*. Its gorgeous plumage and red beak are only superficially Chinese, but it derives its evocative power from association with the winged symbol of Ahura-Mazda, the divine protector of the ancient Achaemenid kings of Iran.

3. The Muraqqa Gulshan

We have already looked at two double-page frontispieces showing Timurid princes taking pleasure in hunting and feasting. Here is another (Plates 16 and 17), from the album known as *Muraqqa Gulshan*, assembled in India about 1610, which depicts a third prince in the intimacy of the harem. There is no doubt as to his identity, for the title "Portrait of Sultan Husayn Mirza," which appears on the book being examined by the two ladies seated in the lower right corner of the composition, agrees with the features and appearance of the only male figure inside the curtained area. Outside, four musicians are seated playing.

The emperor Babur, who knew Herat at the time of Sultan Husayn, records a number of musicians who won fame at his court, but only two artists: Shah Muzaffar, who died young, and Bihzad, who long survived his master. His name completes the inscription on the book in the picture, but it does not appear to be an actual signature, and his

Jami al-Tavarikh. Entertainment in honor of Hulagu, the ruler of Iran, by his brother Monkka (detail). Sixteenth-seventeenth century.

Jami al-Tavarikh. Ghazan Khan, on becoming ruler of Iran, leaves Tabriz (detail). Sixteenth-seventeenth century.

authorship is not unquestioned. Judging from the apparent age of the Sultan, this would be a work of about 1480, when he was fourty-one, or even earlier, which would make it the carliest surviving wok by Bihzad if it were centemporary. The long-rayed visage of the sun is, however, rather in the manner of the early Safavi period (commencing in 1506); but the graceful pattern made by the figures is one of Bihzad's felicities and so are the color harmonies. The strong diagonals of the curtain wall which tie the two halves of the composition together are characteristic of his interest in architectural form. These pages were probably designed as the frontispiece to some work by the Sultan, who was himself a poet, and may well therefore be from a later period of his life than appears at first sight. Such subtle flattery as to show him as he was in his prime is not unknown and would not be unlikely.

The other pages reproduced from the album were all created a generation or more later. The court feasting scene on two facing pages (Plates 18 and 19) can be dated in the 1530s and shows the Safavi style as it was practiced in the first half of Shah Tahmasp's reign. The latter succeeded in 1524 at the age of eleven and the great period of his patronage was between about 1530 and 1545, in which year he renounced the arts as a frivolous waste of time, obliging some of his painters to seek a living elsewhere — Abd al-Samad and Mir Sayyid Ali went to the Mughal emperor Humayun in India about 1550.

Like the other pages now to be mentioned this picture was extended in the early seventeenth century, no doubt when the emperor Jahangir was having them prepared for mounting in his album. One picture actually carries a note by his court painter Daulat to the effect that he had added the hills behind the hunting scene (Plate 22). On the next page from the album a royal party is shown approaching a tent (Plate 21); and this seems to have been twice altered, the first time by Daulat, or one of his fellows, and then again about 1700 when the heavy clouds at the top must have been painted in. The hunting scene and royal cavalcade (Plate 22) seem on the other hand to have been painted about 1525 in Bukhara, where the Shaibanid Uzbeks kept court and supported some of the best Timurid artists from Herat, who preferred to carry on the old tradition rather than follow the line of the new Safavi style.

A night picnic scene is in the gorgeous court style of Tahmasp as it was at its height about 1540 (Plate 23). It might even be by his leading artist Mir Musavvir, but a little heaviness suggests that it is more probably the work of his son, Mir Sayyid Ali, who was to move to India, as we have seen, about ten years later. The façade of the rock-cliff behind the picnic party is built up of a counterpoint of poised crags which cut across the deep blue night sky.

The lower part of the double composition incongruously formed from two distinct sources by the album mounter, and showing Majnun living in his distraction in intimacy with the wild animals (Plate 24), may also be taken from a manuscript of about the same date, illustrated by a pupil of Bihzad working in the new capital Tabriz and preserving more of the feeling of the school of Herat at the end of the fifteenth century. Above, a slight tinted drawing of two men in the court dress of the time of the Emperor Humayun purports to be a work by Abd al-Samad made on the first New Year's day after his summons to India by the emperor in 1550, according to the note written on it in a style which suggests the royal pen of Jahangir or one of his librarians. Even as the work of half a day, as it is said to be, this does not seem worthy of the virtuosity of some of his other signed miniatures on other pages of this album; and it is more probably a work of thirty years later.

4. The Khamsa of Jami

A manuscript of the *Khamsa* (*Five Poems*) of Jami dated 1522 is unusual in being illustrated only by five double-page miniatures (Plate 25 and 26). Each of these pairs carries a "signature," or cartouche, giving the names of pupils of the great Bihzad, who are mentioned in early sources but whose work is otherwise not known to survive. Maqsud, to whom the painting "Sikandar listening to music" (Plate 26) is attributed, is recorded to have carried on, at Herat, the tradition of his master, with great skill in execution but inferior powers of invention. These pages do indeed preserve the Herat style, but in a way more characteristic of the school of Bukhara in about 1540. There, the Uzbek rulers of the Shaibanid house tried to revive the splendors of Timurid patronage in the Herat of Sultan Husayn Bayqara, whose surviving painters and calligraphers they tried to attract to their court. This Bukhara school was remarkable for the clarity of its compositions, often derived from Bihzad himself, but simplified by the omission of some subordinate figures. The miniatures have lost the strong architectural organization of Bihzad's own work and the structural sense is weakened. Charming and gracious rather than dramatic, the school soon becomes monotonous and insipid.

5. The Khamsa of Nizami

The last pair of miniatures is reproduced from a manuscript of Nizami's *Khamsa* in the full Safavi style of the middle of the sixteenth century in the more conservative center of Shiraz. There the taste was for elaborate scenes which leave little space vacant. Figures of bystanders were added even in scenes where they are not very appropriate, such as the denouement of the love story of Layla and Majnun, when the lovers, completely overcome by their emotion, both faint on finally meeting after endless frustration and privations (Plate 27). Spectators at a polo match (Plate 28) are more to be expected, and the two teams of the lovers Khusrau and Shirin in their gay clothes make a satisfying pattern. In both

22

Muraqqa Gulshan. Detail of plate 19.

miniatures, crisscross diagonals form the basis of the compositions, which have a tapestry-like density.

Coming to the work of the sixteenth century from that of the fifteenth, one is aware of the loss of drama, the slackening of emotional engagement, but the essential quality of the whole Persian miniature school remains: its unique union of the romantic and emotional within the compass of the manuscript form. The integrity of the page is preserved, as is, therefore, the close relation between the miniature and the text.

Pascal wrote that there are three gates of perception upon the universe: the sensual, the intellectual, and the emotional. All three avenues are opened in Persian miniatures. Color is employed in its purest tones, while the pigments are the richest available, including gold and silver, lapis lazuli, and malachite. The paper too was prepared with utmost care, and under favorable conditions has remained unchanged for five hundred years. Gold and colored margination of text and illustrations, illuminated headings to each strophe, more elaborate ones for each stanza, and richer still for each poem or book, attest the importance of the book as a work of art. Such sensual pleasure in color and pattern has been the aim of no other school. Persian painting is intellectual in the sense that it places a high value on form, and reflects the figurative language of much Persian poetry, associating the stance of youth with the cypress, the girl's face with the moon, emphasizing the glory of the night sky, the enclosed garden as a setting for love, and using wine as its symbol. But the special characteristic of Persian painting, which sets it apart in the world's art, is its lyrical quality, its power of conveying the emotional charge of a situation, to which both line and color contribute. The color might be merely sensual if it were not combined into the most splendid harmonies, which touch the imagination as well as delight the eye.

ILLUSTRATIONS

1

2

5

9

12

14

15

16

18

19

23